DUNK ISLAND
AND BEAVER CAY

BY

DAVID HEENAN

GLENMEDE

Dunk Island is the largest member of the Family Group of Islands, and a National Park. Purtaboi, the small island in the foreground, is an official Bird Sanctuary.

The panoramic view from the look-out at the top of Mt. Kootaloo, the highest peak on Dunk Island.

Muggy-muggy Beach is just one of several beautiful beaches on Dunk Island.

Some of the 50 game-fishing boats which compete in the Dunk Island Billfish Classic, a game-fishing tournament held each September.

Beautiful Beaver Reef and Cay lie within easy reach of Dunk Island.

Author and photographer, David Heenan.

PUBLISHED BY
GLENMEDE PTY. LTD.

P.O. BOX 291, RED HILL, QUEENSLAND, AUSTRALIA 4059
TELEPHONE: 018-545 901

FIRST PUBLISHED 1994

National Library of Australia
Card Number ISBN 0 646 16849 5

ACKNOWLEDGEMENTS

The photographs in this book were taken by David Heenan with the exception of those listed below.

The author would like to thank the individuals and organisations who provided this additional material.

UNDERWATER PHOTOGRAPHY
Peter Harrison. Plates 1/2, pg. 40; plate 3, pg. 41.
Ian Mariner. Plate 1, pg. 41.
Bill Wood. All images, pgs. 46/7.

OTHER PHOTOGRAPHS
Lincoln Fowler. Plate 1, pgs. 6/7; plate 1, pg. 36; plate 1, pg. 38.
Grahame Walsh. Plates 1/2, pg. 20.
Cliff & Dawn Frith. Plates 1/2, pg. 30; plates 1/2, pg. 31.
Australian Resorts. Plate 2, Front Cover; plate 3, pg. 36; plates 1-3, pg. 37.

HISTORICAL PHOTOGRAPHS
National Library of Australia. Plates 1-3, pg. 18; plate 1, pg. 19.
John Hopkins. Plate 1, pg. 21; plate 2, pg. 24; plate 1, pg. 25.
John Oxley Library. Plate 1, pg. 22; plate 1, pg. 23; plate 1, pg. 24; plate 2, pg. 25.

PRINTED BY INPRINT, BRISBANE

People swim, snorkel and dive at Beaver Cay.

Contents

This Swing-bridge crosses a small ravine in the heart of Dunk's lush rainforest.

DUNK ISLAND
AND BEAVER CAY

Dunk Island, which is on the same latitude as Fiji, is undoubtedly one of Australia's best-known islands.

Many people in Australia and overseas learned about it decades ago through articles and books written by Edmund Banfield, who lived a secluded life on the island between 1897 and 1923. He wrote four books about his life on the island, the first and perhaps most famous being "Confessions of a Beachcomber".

Of all the continental islands within the Great Barrier region Dunk Island is one of the most tropical in terms of vegetation. A large area of the island is covered in dense jungle but there are also eucalypt forests, grassy areas and mangrove flats. The landscape includes hills and valleys, cliffs and precipices, rocky promontories, sandy beaches and small coves.

Dunk Island lies about 160 kilometres north of Townsville and 120 kilometres south of Cairns. It is six kilometres long and about two kilometres wide at its broadest point.

The summer temperatures on the island range between 23°C and 31°C, and the winter temperatures are between 17°C and 26°C.

Most of Dunk Island is now classified as a National Park and visitors can explore much of its beautiful rainforest on excellent tracks maintained by the National Parks and Wildlife Service.

Over 150 different species of birds have been recorded on the island. Another winged resident is the brilliant blue Papilio Ulysses butterfly, which has been adopted as a symbol for Dunk Island.

Aborigines once lived on Dunk Island. The tribe was known as the Djiru and their name for the island was Coonanglebah.

The island received its present name from Captain James Cook. He named it after Lord George Montagu Dunk, Earl of Halifax and First Lord of the British Admiralty.

In 1969 the movie "The Age of Consent", starring James Mason, was filmed here as well as on nearby Bedarra Island.

Today, the island is a popular destination for visitors. The resort on the island has been long established and caters for up to 400 guests. About two thirds of the guests are Australians with the rest coming from overseas, mostly from the United States and Europe. Apart from water sports the resort has a golf course, tennis courts and horse riding.

Visitors to Dunk Island also enjoy easy access to the Outer Reef – visiting Beaver Cay and coral gardens around it that abound with colourful marine life.

DUNK ISLAND

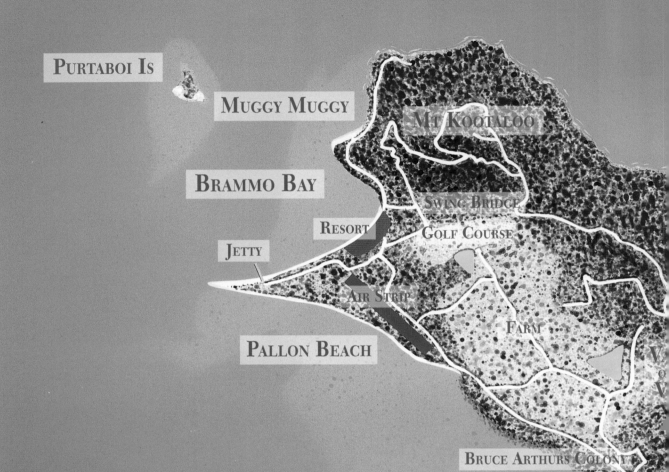

PURTABOI IS

MUGGY MUGGY

MT KOOTALOO

BRAMMO BAY

SWING BRIDGE

RESORT

GOLF COURSE

JETTY

AIR STRIP

FARM

PALLON BEACH

BRUCE ARTHURS COLONY

MANGUM GNACKUM IS

THE FAMILY GROUP OF ISLANDS

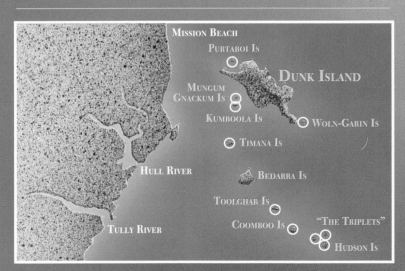

MISSION BEACH

PURTABOI IS

DUNK ISLAND

MUNGUM
GNACKUM IS

KUMBOOLA IS

WOLN-GARIN IS

TIMANA IS

HULL RIVER

BEDARRA IS

TOOLGHAR IS

TULLY RIVER

COOMBOO IS

"THE TRIPLETS"

HUDSON IS

KUMBOOLA IS

AUSTRALIA

ATIONAL PARK

PALM VALLEY

COCONUT BAY

WOLN-GARIN IS

N

"The Endeavour" which sailed through the Family Group in 1770.

Captain Cook named Dunk Island on June 8, 1770.

The "HMS Rattlesnake" which surveyed the Family Group in 1848.

DUNK ISLAND is one of a dozen islands within a group named the Family Islands.

James Cook encountered the islands and named the group as he threaded his way northwards in 1770. According to his Journals he passed through them on June 8 of that year. He noted that "we saw on one of the nearest Islands a Number of the Natives collected together, who seem'd to look very attentively upon the Ship; they were quite naked, and of a very Dark Colour, with short hair".

Cook passed Dunk on the eastern or seaward side. It is obvious that Cook considered it to be the most appealing island within the Family Group because it was the only individual one that he named. Cook named it after his patron, Lord George Montagu Dunk, Earl of Halifax, Earl of Sandwich and First Lord of the British Admiralty.

Born a Montagu, this canny nobleman exchanged his illustrious name for that of his wife's rather undistinguished one. He chose to do so for the very simple reason that inheritance of her father's rather impressive fortune depended on it.

Lord Montagu Dunk also invented the humble sandwich. He was such a passionate gambler that he created the sandwich to ensure that as little time as possible would be wasted on meals.

The next visit to Dunk of any note was in May, 1848, by the warship HMS "Rattlesnake", under the command of Captain Owen Stanley. The "Rattlesnake" was, in fact, the escort for the "Tam O' Shanter" which carried the well-known explorer Edmund Kennedy. Kennedy was deposited on the mainland opposite to Dunk Island to begin what became a fateful overland expedition.

ONCE INHABITED BY ABORIGINES.

John MacGillivray, the naturalist aboard the "Rattlesnake", spent 10 days on Dunk Island. As his party explored the northern part of the island trouble erupted. Two of the young "gentlemen" in MacGillivray's party went on a hunting trip and approached a native camp a little too closely. When the aborigines tried to resist their advance the two white men fired shots at them. The aborigines fled but did not forget the incident.

From that point onwards the natives of Dunk Island developed a treacherous reputation. The island natives were a very independent people who had virtually no contact with mainland tribes. They enjoyed a plentiful supply of sea-food and clearly regarded the arrival of white men in their domain as a most unwelcome intrusion.

One well documented incident occurred in 1877. On January 18, the men aboard a schooner called either the "Thomas Hardy" or "Thomas Harris" sailed from Cairns to Dunk Island. The purpose of the trip was to collect wood for their Bêche-de-mer boilers.

When they arrived at Dunk Island the schooner moored about half a mile off-shore and two of the crew members –

John MacGillivray, a naturalist aboard "HMS Rattlesnake", spent 10 days exploring Dunk Island.

Humphrey Coughland and Alexander MacIntosh – were put in charge of a hut on the island.

The following morning Harris, the skipper of the schooner, was aroused by a loud cry. Harris immediately went up on deck where he found a member of his crew dying from a wound in the head.

An article in an early edition of the "Australasian Encyclopaedia" vividly describes the dramatic events that followed. "Looking up, he saw a blackfellow stalking the mate. When he shouted a warning, the native then attacked the captain with the half-axe he was carrying".

Harris was wounded but he managed to retreat to the safety of his cabin where he kept his revolver. Harris, however, had difficulty loading the weapon because of the severe wound that he had suffered.

"In the meantime other blacks had arrived and were trying to break the cabin door with their half-axes. The captain managed at length to load the revolver, and he fired a shot through the skylight. Hearing the shot, John Shaw – a seaman – broke his way through the lazarette door.

Blacks were cutting and hacking at everything they could reach, and the steward who got in their way was half-scalped before he could crawl away to join the captain and the others in the cabin.

The captain now had two men to lead against half a dozen blacks. They made the charge and two blacks were killed in the first encounter. After a further struggle the rest of the blacks were killed or driven into the water.

Harris then found the bodies of two seamen hacked to pieces. Coughland and MacIntosh were both found murdered in their hut on Dunk Island…"

Another bloody incident occurred on Dunk Island the following year. This took place some time after a steamer called the "Merchant", carrying a cargo of cedar, left Port Hinchinbrook to head south.

This ship – which had just been repaired after running aground on a shoal – then had the misfortune to find itself at sea when a bad cyclone hit the Queensland coast. The "Merchant" was totally wrecked on this occasion and the crew were never seen again.

The wreckage of the doomed vessel, however, was found over a very wide area. The enterprising crew of one salvage boat subsequently arrived at Dunk Island searching for the remains of the "Merchant's" valuable cargo. They scoured the island's beaches until they encountered some of the local and hostile natives. The crew suffered wounds and bruises but were lucky enough to escape.

Some of the cedar from the "Merchant" actually lay on Dunk's beaches for almost 20 years until E.J. Banfield took up residence on the island. He salvaged at least one log and used the timber in building a punt as well as different items of furniture for his home.

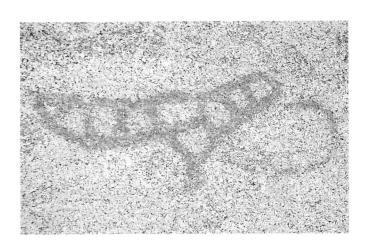

A number of primitive aboriginal rock paintings have been discovered on Dunk Island. A visitor to Dunk Island in 1866 estimated that 400 aborigines were living on the island at that time.

E.J. Banfield, a journalist turned beachcomber.

Living on a tropical island has long been considered a romantic dream. What person has not read the exploits of the shipwrecked Robinson Crusoe without feeling somewhat envious of his unencumbered life?

Whilst Robinson Crusoe was a fictitious character, however, Edmund J. Banfield was not. And whilst the former was eventually rescued and returned to "civilization", the latter loved Dunk Island so much that he lived on it happily until his death.

Edmund J. Banfield was born in Liverpool in 1852. He left England for Australia in 1854, along with his two sisters and a brother, under the care of his mother. His father, Jabez W. Banfield, had already migrated to this country ahead of the family.

After joining several rushes to the goldfields Jabez Banfield helped found a newspaper in Maryborough, Victoria. In 1857, Banfield senior took his family to Ararat where he ran another newspaper. It was here that his son Edmund also began a career in journalism. Edmund Banfield worked later in Sydney as a journalist and then, in 1882, took the rather adventuresome step of moving to far-off Townsville. He worked with the "Townsville Daily Bulletin" for 15 years, until he became desperately ill through overwork and exhaustion.

In September, 1896, Banfield camped on the beach of Dunk Island with his wife Bertha and a few friends. Banfield, who had previously absorbed the writings of Thoreau, the American philosopher who advocated a life close to nature, was immediately captivated by the thought of living on this beautiful island.

Banfield subsequently managed to lease a small area of Dunk Island for a period of 30 years at an annual rental of two shillings and sixpence an acre, and later secured a larger freehold block.

When the Banfields arrived on Dunk to take up permanent residence in 1897 they were greeted by Tom, an aborigine who they had become acquainted with on their first visit. Tom helped the Banfields unload their many provisions and worked for them on and off for many years. Unfortunately, the attractions of rum and opium prompted Tom to travel regularly to the mainland. On one visit he died after being speared by his half-brother during a drunken fight.

After their arrival the Banfields lived in tents for only a short time since Edmund had had the foresight to ship a prefabricated hut to the island. This was made out of cedar and "so contrived with nicely adjusting parts and bolts, and all its members numbered, that a mere amateur could put it together." On Banfield's own admission it also had the advantage of being easily dismantled if life happened to become unendurable on Dunk Island.

Despite the many different hardships of becoming almost completely self-sufficient, Banfield found Dunk a joyful place to live. "Scent and silence," he wrote, "is the phrase which

E.J. Banfield lived the life of a Beachcomber on Dunk Island between 1897 and 1923.

expresses the individuality of our island and better 'scented silence' than all the noisy odours of the town."

For six years this small hut sheltered the Banfields, and the occasional bat, until a larger bungalow was built. Over four acres were also cleared as a plantation for fruit and vegetables including bananas, oranges, pawpaws, pineapples, custard apples, melons, sweet potatoes, maize, strawberries, herbs and even coffee.

The sea provided food, too. There were oysters for the taking, crabs from the mangrove flats and an abundant supply of fresh fish. In addition, the Banfields had a few poultry as well as cows and goats which provided milk and fresh meat. They also arranged for a coastal steamer that passed the island weekly to drop off any supplies needed from the outside world and any mail for them.

Although there were many back-breaking chores to be done each day, Banfield still had time to contemplate and study nature. Indeed, he acquired a remarkable knowledge of the teeming wild-life on Dunk Island and meticulously recorded it.

To finance the few supplies they needed from the outside world, Banfield wrote articles about life on Dunk Island for newspapers and journals under the whimsical pen-name of Rob Krusoe. Ten years after arriving on Dunk Island his first book "Confessions of a Beachcomber" was also published.

This volume was followed by "My Tropic Isle", "Tropic Days" and "Last Leaves from Dunk". In colourful prose, Banfield shared the secrets of nature that he had uncovered, wrote about the legends and often macabre customs of the local aborigines, and told many engrossing stories of his own experiences as well as those of visitors.

One local aboriginal legend he recorded tells the story of how the Southern Cross constellation originated. Long ago two aboriginal fishermen speared a huge shovel-nosed shark whilst they were fishing off Dunk Island in their canoe. The speared shark, named Dooey-dooey, dived – capsizing the canoe and throwing the two men into the water.

Dooey-dooey then dragged the canoe through the water by the harpoon rope. The two men tried in vain to catch the canoe, swimming in pursuit from Dunk Island as far as Magnetic Island and then out to the Great Barrier Reef and over the horizon of the South Pacific, all to no avail. They can still be seen – Dooey-dooey and the canoe (forming the cross) and the two men following behind (the two stars alpha and beta Centauri).

In "Confessions of a Beachcomber" Banfield also tells how the local aborigines would capture a large turtle. They would first catch a "sucker" fish, which has the ability of pressing a disc with ridges on the upper part of its body against a smooth surface and then forming a vacuum in between. This would be fastened to a light line until a turtle was sighted from a canoe.

The "sucker" fish would then be thrown in the turtle's direction to which it would inevitably attach itself. The aborigines would then play the turtle until it was exhausted. Sometimes this

Bertha Banfield, the Beachcomber's cheerful and faithful companion.

would take an hour or more and the patient natives would on occasions be towed seven or eight kilometres out to sea before it tired. The turtle would then be harpooned, hauled alongside, and towed ashore – no mean task in a fragile bark canoe.

Turtles can still be seen in the waters around Dunk Island and, sometimes, a dugong. This harmless creature, commonly known as a "sea cow", looks like a cross between a hippopotamus and a seal. This "strange, paradoxical mammal", as Banfield described it, grazes on sea grass.

Banfield's books were read around Australia and overseas and they brought him fame and mail from right around the globe. Letters came from children, one writing that Dunk would undoubtedly be "a fine place to play Indians!". Others came from professors and even from a group of prisoners in an American penitentiary. Banfield also received letters from would-be Crusoes and some even arrived unannounced.

Mention should be made as well of Bertha Banfield, his "merry little wife". She was always a cheerful and uncomplaining companion for Edmund throughout the many lonely years they spent together on Dunk Island.

Since she had no children, the only other company Bertha had was Essie, an Irishwoman, who was an "assistant" to the Banfields from 1904. Essie had previously worked for them when they had lived in Townsville.

Unfortunately, Essie was visiting Townsville when Edmund Banfield died of appendicitis on June 2, 1923. Bertha was alone on Dunk Island with her husband's body for three days until she was able to attract the attention of a passing steamer, the "Innisfail".

An 18-year old steward on the steamer saw her waving a sheet on the beach. At first this was interpreted as a greeting. Then she collapsed on the beach and those on board realised there was something amiss. A party was then despatched ashore where they heard of Banfield's death.

After making a coffin, the crew of the steamer laid Banfield to rest in his own garden with Captain Robertson reading the burial service.

A stone cairn still marks the spot (which is just a short distance from the resort on Dunk Island). It bears the following inscription: "If a man does not keep pace with his companions, perhaps it is because he hears a different drummer. Let him step to the music he hears."

Bertha remained on Dunk Island with Essie for another year. Then, perhaps to make up for the many years she had spent in isolation on the island, she travelled and lived in Queensland, New South Wales and Victoria.

Bertha outlived her husband by 10 years. When she died in 1933, her ashes were deposited beneath the cairn that marked the final resting place of Edmund Banfield.

Interest in Edmund Banfield still remains high. His books have been reprinted and the Royal Queensland Theatre Company recently produced a play about his life.

The Banfield's first home on the island.

Edmund J. Banfield and his wife lie buried together on their tropical island.

The second, larger home built by the Banfield's. (Photographed in 1936.)

The Beachcomber sits in the stern of his boat "Yan-O-Lee".

Edmund Banfield shares the verandah of his home with an unknown guest.

"Red Wing" visits Brammo Bay in 1930.

Ferns abound in the lush rainforest.

A Bird's Nest Fern.

The buttressed trunk of a tall rainforest tree.

The dense rainforest canopy on Dunk Island.

Delicate fungi defy gravity.

Good walking trails traverse the island.

THE name given to Dunk Island originally by the local aborigines was "Coonanglebah" which means Isle of Peace and Plenty. It is indeed a tranquil place – and there is plenty to see.

One of the delights of Dunk Island are the walks that you can take through its dense rainforest. The National Parks and Wildlife Service maintain a number of excellent walking trails on the island and these enable you to thoroughly explore the western half of the island.

The more rugged eastern half of Dunk Island is inaccessible by foot but visitors have the opportunity of seeing the small coves and beaches on this side by boat. (Small aluminium boats can be rented from the resort's Watersport Shed).

"ISLE OF PEACE AND PLENTY"

Many strange shapes can be seen in the rainforest.

A short but very enjoyable walk is the one to Muggy-muggy Bay. This secluded cove lies north of Brammo Bay where the resort is situated and takes not much longer than 15 minutes to reach. The track runs parallel to the water and along the way you'll see a rich variety of vegetation including Paperbark and Umbrella trees, and many Maidenhair and Bird's Nest ferns.

Another walk which is well worth the effort is the one to the top of Dunk's highest peak, Mt. Kootaloo, which is 271 metres above sea level. Almost at the outset of the walk you pass the grave of Edmund Banfield. Shortly afterwards you will cross a small ravine via a swing bridge and then the track becomes like a tunnel through dense, verdant rainforest.

The return trip to Mt. Kootaloo takes around two hours. All the way you will travel through lush rainforest of towering trees forming a green canopy overhead with countless palms, ferns and small plants at ground level.

One of the small creatures you may encounter on your walks is the Echidna. They were known to the aborigines that once inhabited Dunk as "Coom-bee-yan" and were regarded by them as a delicacy.

This shy creature is, in fact, a spiny ant-eater. Banfield described it as "an animal which possesses some of the features of the hedgehog of Old England, and resembles in others that distinctly Australian paradox, the platypus".

Muggy-muggy Beach, aboriginal for "Coral mushroom where crayfish lurk".

As you near the highest point of Mt. Kootaloo you will get a spectacular view of Brammo Bay and the mainland in the distance. From a look-out almost at the very top of Mt. Kootaloo you will enjoy panoramic views over some of the other members of the Family group of islands.

At the summit of Mt. Kootaloo, just a few metres away from this look-out, are the remains of a radar station. During World War II this played a vital role in monitoring the Battle of the Coral Sea.

If you walk in a south-easterly direction from the resort you will find yourself not in dense rainforest but in the open fields of a farm where horses are kept for horse-riding.

Beyond the farm on Dunk Island there is also a small colony of artists. The walk to this interesting settlement will take you about half an hour. Twenty minutes further on you will find Coconut Beach, a long sandy beach fringed by trees. A feature of this beach are the beautiful Callophylum trees, more commonly known as Cyclone trees. These grow as high as 20 metres, have very low lying foliage and can be very old.

A circular trail will actually take you to Coconut Beach and back to the resort via Mt. Kootaloo if you wish. If you choose this longer route rather than simply backtracking you should allow about five hours for the round trip.

Another destination worth visiting is Purtaboi, the small rocky

Purtaboi Island – which lies directly off Brammo Bay – is an official Bird Sanctuary.

island lying directly off-shore from the resort at Brammo Bay.

Edmund Banfield described it as "dainty and unique – its hill crowned with low-growing trees and shrubs, a ruddy precipice, groups of Pandanus palms, beach lined with Casuarinas, (with) banks of snow-white coral debris…"

This little island was close to where the HMS "Rattlesnake" anchored in May, 1848, and served as a station for Captain Stanley when he determined various astronomical positions.

Apart from birdwatching you can also enjoy both swimming and snorkelling. Purtaboi has a small but beautiful sandy beach and if you like picnics, it's a wonderful spot to have one. To get to Purtaboi simply hire a boat at the Watersports shed.

The Azure Kingfisher feeds on crustaceans, fish and water insects.

Spectacled Monarchs live on insects like ants and spiders.

Metallic Starlings, which nest during August and September, feed on the fruit of rainforest trees.

A Reef Heron or Egret.

Black-naped Terns feed on small fish.

During his life on the island, Banfield recorded dozens of species of birds on Dunk Island. In fact, over a hundred different species have been sighted on Dunk and nearby Purtaboi since records have been kept.

Even if you're not normally an avid birdwatcher still consider packing a pair of binoculars for this purpose should you decide to visit Dunk Island. Most people develop an instant interest in the bird-life they suddenly find around them because of the many unusual varieties, colours and calls of these feathered inhabitants.

During the months of June and July you should also see many butterflies flitting gaily through the rainforest, including the spectacular Ulysses which is vibrant blue in colour. This has a wingspan of around four inches or 10 centimetres, making it one of Australia's largest butterflies.

For those people interested, the impressive list of birds that can be seen around Dunk Island includes the Pelican, Little Grebe, Little Pied Cormorant, Pied Cormorant, White-faced Heron, Reef Heron, Mangrove Heron, Nankeen Night Heron, White Ibis, Straw-necked Ibis, Brown Goshawk, Whistling Kite, Black Kite, Brahminy Kite, Wedge-tailed Eagle, White-breasted Sea Eagle, Osprey, Beach Stone-Curlew, Red-Capped Dotterel, plus five varieties of both terns and pigeons.

Other varieties are the Silver Gull, Sulphur-crested Cockatoo, Rainbow Lorikeet, Peregrine Falcon, Scrub-Fowl, Brush Turkey, Rednecked Rail, Grey Plover, Whimbril, Eastern Curlew, Masked Plover, Common Sandpiper, Grey-tailed Tattler, Dusky Honeyeater, Spice Finch, Shining Starling, Yellow Oriole, Spangled Drongo, Yellow Figbird, Southern Figbird, Masked Wood-swallow, White-breasted Wood-swallow, Pied Currawong, Rainbow Bird, Dollar Bird, Shining Bronze Cuckoo, Laughing Kookaburra, Blue-winged Kookaburra, Pheasant Coucal, Channel-billed Cuckoo, Koel and Barn Owl.

Four species of the striking Kingfisher family have been sighted – the Azure Kingfisher, Forest Kingfisher, Mangrove Kingfisher and Sacred Kingfisher.

Other species – many with fanciful names – include the White-tailed Nightjar, Welcome Swallow, Tree Martin, Grey Swiftlet, Noisy Pitta, Magpie-Lark, Brown Songlark, Australian Pipit, Varied Triller, White-winged Triller, Little Cuckoo-skrike, Black-faced Cuckoo-shrike, Large-billed Warbler, Grey Fantail, Rufous Fantail and six species of the Flycatcher.

To complete this extensive list there is the Rufous Shrike-thrush, Bower Shrike-thrush, Mistletoe Bird, Yellow-breasted Sunbird and the Grey-breasted Silvereye.

If you are interested in the island's bird-life you can join a special birdwatch tour organised by the resort once a week.

Purtaboi, the small island which lies directly off Brammo Bay, is an official bird sanctuary.

Birds that nest on Purtaboi Island include Torres Strait or Nutmeg Pigeons, Doves, Honey-eaters, Reef Herons, Cormorants and Large-billed Shore Plovers.

COLOUR IN FLIGHT

A Blue Triangle Butterfly sips the nectar of a flower.

The brilliant Ulysses Butterfly, one of Australia's largest and most colourful butterflies, can be seen on Dunk.

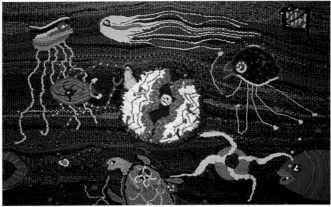
A tapestry by Bruce Arthur.

"The Dome" houses work that visitors can purchase.

A painting by one of the local artists.

Julie Wall, who creates pottery and sculpture, stands outside her

Susie Kirk, a Silversmith, outside her mud-brick house.

Some of the jewellery Susie has created.

O<small>N</small> the southern side of Dunk Island, about half an hour's walk from the resort, is a small artists' colony. This was founded in 1974 by Bruce Arthur.

Bruce was once a wrestler who participated in the 1948 London Olympics. He then wrestled professionally. Tiring of this career, and influenced by the writings of David Thoreau, a philospher who advocated a simple, unencumbered life close to nature, Bruce decided to move to Queensland's tropical north.

Bruce initially settled on Timana Island, a small island close by to Dunk Island – and it was here that he began his artistic life as a weaver. After nine years, Bruce moved to Dunk Island and since then his work has brought him national acclaim.

small home called "Robin's Nest".

Bruce Arthur, the founder of the community, weaves tapestries with wool he has dyed himself.

Many of his tapestries hang in the foyers of grand hotels and theatres. A lot of Bruce's tapestries have also been commissioned by well-known Australian artists such as Clifton Pugh and Fred Williams. They visit or send Bruce detailed designs and he then weaves them using wool specially dyed by himself.

Bruce lives in a mud-brick house which he built himself. Additional dwellings were built to house other artists who came to learn the craft of weaving. The small community has also been a retreat for potters, sculptors, painters and silversmiths.

Visitors staying on Dunk Island can visit the small colony twice a week. Tapestries, pottery, painting, and jewellery made by Bruce Arthur and other local artists can be purchased.

THE RESORT

Tourists started to visit Dunk Island as far back as 1934. Banfield's old bungalow provided the accommodation for those first guests. The "resort" was owned by Spencer Hopkins of Townsville and managed by the George Morris family.

Noel Wood, who lived on nearby Bedarra Island for some 50 years, occasionally helped out at the resort and remembers those early days. Dinner was often braised turtle accompanied by a bottle of claret (ten pence a bottle).

Draught beer from Cairns and different brands of bottled beer from Melbourne were served – including Melbourne Bitter, Abbotts and Fosters. There were no refrigerators back then, of course, and the beer was stored in concrete boxes with

Dunk Island's resort is situated at beautiful Brammo Bay.

ice. The labels inevitably floated off in the water from the melting ice and the barman simply slapped the nearest label onto the nearest bottle. None of the customers seemed to notice or complain, Noel remembers with good humour. Much has changed since those early days.

The resort has passed through different hands but since 1978 it has been owned by Australian Resorts, a division of Qantas Airlines, and they have continually up-graded it.

The modern resort – which accommodates up to 400 guests – is set in tropical gardens with a profusion of brilliant Bougainvillea, Hibiscus, Frangipani, purple Bauhinia and many other beautiful and colourful plants. The gardens are kept in their beautiful state by a horticulturalist and eight gardeners.

The standard of the main facilities is excellent and there is a range of accommodation for all budgets. There are four types of accommodation – luxury Bayview Villas which are set right on the beach; spacious Beachfront Units which overlook the beach; slightly smaller Banfield Units and Garden Cabanas.

All forms of accommodation have private bathrooms, air-conditioning, and mini-bars.

Guests have a choice of two restaurants – the casual, tropical atmosphere of the Beachcomber Restaurant which overlooks beautiful Brammo Bay and the smaller more formal Rainforest Brasserie.

Several of the jockeys prepare for the Dunk Island Cup.

Horses race along the main Brammo Bay beach. The event is staged every year on Melbourne Cup Day.

Breakfast and lunch are served buffet style in the Beachcomber Restaurant and in the evenings there is a menu that changes daily. If you love seafood then you will certainly look forward to Friday nights. In the evening a wonderful seafood banquet is served in the Beachcomber Restaurant. Guests are treated to a mammoth smorgasbord of lobster, prawns, mud crabs, reef fish and oysters.

The smaller Brasserie offers a menu of fine dishes and waitress service for both lunch and dinner.

Both restaurants have a good selection of quality Australian white wines and reds to complement your meal.

After the evening meal, there is always live entertainment.

Long John, the Race Steward, suitably dressed for the tropics!

There is a resident band and guest artists play occasionally.

An evening child-minding service is available for those with children. There is even a special dinner at 5:30 p.m. every night for children over the age of three. During the day children have their own activities centre staffed by two or three adults.

Guests staying at the resort have many activities to choose from during the day. Apart from swimming, windsurfing and catamaran sailing you will find a 6-hole golf course, clay target shooting, an archery range, horse-riding, tandem sky-diving, aerobics, softball, beach volleyball, basquetball, cricket, touch football, badminton and tennis courts. There are also air-conditioned squash courts.

Guests explore Dunk on horse back.

The resort offers four grades of accommodation.

Dunk has its own 6-hole golf course.

The use of all sports facilities and most equipment is free. Only tandem sky-diving, horse riding, clay target shooting and activities which use fuel – such as water-skiing and parasailing – are extra.

Resort facilities include a boutique with a wide range of items including casual wear, swimwear, toiletries, books, magazines, newspapers, postcards and stamps (there is a daily postal service) and a 24-hour film processing service. The resort even has a hairdressing salon.

For those guests who can't wait for mealtimes there is the Jetty Cafe as well, which serves hot and cold snacks, ice-creams and cool drinks.

The management really have thought of everything to make your stay as enjoyable and relaxing as possible. Along with the natural beauty of Dunk Island and a tropical lushness that few other islands can match it's hardly surprising that it is one of the most popular destinations within the Great Barrier Reef region.

How to get to Dunk Island.

To visit Dunk Island you have several options. There are daily flights between Townsville and the island, and flights from Cairns every day. Flights from both Townsville and Cairns to Dunk take about 40 minutes.

If you are travelling by road on the mainland you can travel

Dunk's Cascade Pool.

There is live entertainment each night in the main lounge.

Luxury accommodation in the resort's Beachfront Villas.

across to Dunk Island by boat. There is a regular ferry service operated by Quickcat Cruises from the Clump Point jetty and water taxis also run regularly from South Mission Beach and Wongaling Beach.

Should you wish to contact the resort at Dunk Island their address is P.M.B. 28, Townsville, QLD 4810. Their phone and facsimile number is (070) 688199 and (070) 688528 respectively.

At the end of Brammo Bay there is a small camping site. Camping permits must be obtained prior to arrival, however, from the National Parks and Wildlife Service. These can be obtained from their Cardwell office. The phone number of the N.P.W.S. at Cardwell is (070) 668601.

The Family Group can be explored aboard the "Neptunius".

Passengers swim and snorkel at Hudson Island.

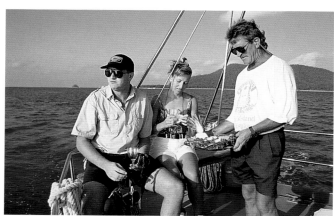

A pleasant way to spend a day.

DUNK is the largest island within The Family Group. In all, there are 16 islands of varying sizes in this picturesque group, all within visible proximity of each other.

Although the islands each have English names, they also have Aboriginal names for this was an area where aborigines lived, hunted and fished up until the beginning of this century. They travelled from island to island in bark canoes.

Apart from Dunk Island, which was the only one in the group named by Captain Cook in 1770, the remaining islands received their English names from Lieutenant G.E. Richards. He surveyed the group aboard HMS "Paluma" in 1886 and named the other islands in honour of officers aboard the vessel. This explains why they have names like Wheeler, Bowden, Coombe and Thorpe.

Today, only several of the islands are inhabited – Dunk, Bedarra and Timana.

Bedarra Island is the only other island that accommodates visitors. There are two small, exclusive resorts at opposite ends of the island – both operated by Australian Resorts, the same company that runs the resort on Dunk Island.

Both resorts on Bedarra cater to just over 30 guests each and attract people seeking great privacy and seclusion. The small, secluded resorts are favourite hideaways for Royalty, Heads of State, tycoons and well-known personalities. The Duchess of York, Dolly Parton, Tony Randall of "The Odd Couple", Art Garfunkel and Sir James Ramsay, Governor of Queensland, have all holidayed on Bedarra Island.

Long before the resorts existed, Bedarra was home to a modern Robinson Crusoe, Noel Wood, an artist with paintings hanging in galleries and private collections all over the world.

Noel Wood led a hermit-like existence on the island from the mid-1930's until 1993. He rarely left the island – although he did help out from time to time at Dunk's resort in the 1940's. He also spent several years in Ireland and Hollywood art directing in films in the early 1950's.

Escaping to Bedarra and buying a third of the island for just 15 pounds in 1935 to live and paint "in his own paradise", Noel Wood became completely self-sufficient – growing his own food and even eating the flowers off bean plants. Despite his isolation from so-called civilisation, Noel was surprisingly well informed and had a great sense of humour.

Thorpe or Timana Island is the only other inhabited island within the Family Group. Deanna Conti, another acclaimed artist and weaver, lives on this tiny island.

Guests staying on Dunk have the opportunity of exploring the Family Group for a complete day aboard the "Neptunius", a magnificent 52' yacht.

Apart from sailing past the various islands, several hours are spent by her passengers picnicking, swimming and snorkelling at Hudson – a small, beautiful island at the very southern end of the group.

Nearby Bedarra, a favourite hideaway of the rich and famous.

Noel Wood, the hermit who lived on Bedarra for over 50 years.

THE OUTER REEF

DUNK ISLAND lies within Australia's Great Barrier Reef region which stretches down the north-eastern coast of Australia for some 2,500 kilometres. The Reef region covers approximately 350,000 square kilometres, making it greater in size than the United Kingdom, and half the size of Texas.

Scattered throughout this entire area is an intricate maze of submerged reefs, beautiful coral cays and a large number of continental islands, most of which are surrounded by their own fringing reefs. Dunk is one such island. Like other continental islands within the region, it was once a mountain peak on the coastline of Australia. When sea levels rose after the last Ice Age, islands like Dunk were formed and coral reefs have developed around many of them.

Whilst Dunk has a fringing reef, visitors can see the most spectacular marine life at nearby Beaver and Taylor Reefs. Both have small, sandy coral cays where guests can sunbathe, picnic, swim and snorkel.

Cays like Beaver and Taylor are normally created as coral debris accumulates at the sheltered or western side of the reef that it sits on (the prevailing winds on the Reef come from the north-east and south-east).

HOW REEFS ARE FORMED.

The Great Barrier Reef is the largest structure ever created on earth by living organisms. The principal engineers of this vast labyrinth of reefs are organisms so small that they are barely visible to the human eye.

These tiny animals are called coral polyps and in hard corals, each polyp builds an external, cup-like skeleton of calcium carbonate. As a founder polyp constantly divides a coral colony is formed. Most coral polyps reproduce by spawning annually following a full moon in October or November.

Many corals are hermaphrodites which means that a single polyp produces both sperm and eggs. The eggs released by polyps vary in colour from bright pinks and reds to blues and greens.

Different corals grow at different rates. Staghorn corals can grow as much as 20 to 30 centimetres a year. Other corals can grow as little as three millimetres in the same period.

Corals feed on microscopic animals floating in the water around them. They catch these minute animals by using tentacles which are armed with barbed darts of stinging cells (fortunately, the stinging darts of most corals have little effect on humans because our skin is too thick for them to penetrate).

The many beautiful colours of live corals are produced by pigments in the outer layers of coral tissue, and by the minute zooxanthellae plant cells and other algae found in their skeletons. Together, the pigments and algae can give corals brilliant colours such as red, green and yellow.

As hard corals die, they are cemented together by their own limestone. As this process is repeated, a reef many metres thick is gradually built up with living corals on its surface pro-

Spawning Brain Coral releases eggs.

Staghorn corals can grow as much as 30 centimetres a year.

viding shelter and food for countless fish, starfish, molluscs and other animals and plants.

SECRETS THAT MAY BENEFIT MANKIND.

In recent times, scientists have been collecting and analysing chemical compounds such as those released by soft corals in the hope that they may have important medicinal qualities.

The Reef may provide many benefits to mankind. Scientists, for instance, are now investigating the mucus produced by corals. This substance shields corals from the detrimental effects of ultra-violet rays and scientists believe it could lead to the development of a much better sun screen to protect humans.

The Reef is home to 1,500 species of fish.

Beaver Reef is one of the 3,000 individual reefs that make up the Great Barrier Reef.

The discovery of this UV blocking agent is also of interest to commercial manufacturers of products like plastics and paints.

A WORLD HERITAGE SITE.

The Great Barrier Reef was declared a World Heritage Site on October 26, 1981. Its protection is the responsibility of the Federally funded Great Barrier Reef Marine Park Authority.

Activities prohibited within the Park include oil exploration, mining, spearfishing with Scuba gear, and the taking of certain specimens of fish or shell species.

The day-to-day management of the Marine Park is entrusted to Queensland's Department of Environment and Conservation.

Nudibranchs or sea slugs come in many amazing colours.

Sea-birds nest each year on coral cays such as Beaver Cay.

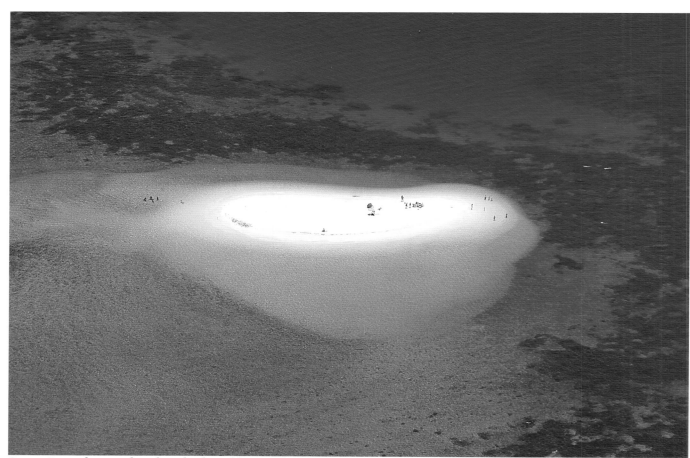

Beaver Cay with its coral gardens clearly visible around it.

"Quickcat" with its glass bottom boat.

Their rangers patrol the Marine Park aboard aircraft and boats monitoring the Reef and its marine life, in order to preserve its rich resources for future generations.

VISITING BEAVER CAY.

A large, fast and comfortable 24 metre motor catamaran whisks visitors out to Beaver Cay every day, weather permitting.

The boat trip out to the Reef aboard "Quickcat" takes just 55 minutes. Once there, you spend a few hours at Beaver Cay and the reef around it.

Here you can snorkel or view its coral gardens and marine life from a glass bottom boat or semi-submersible craft without

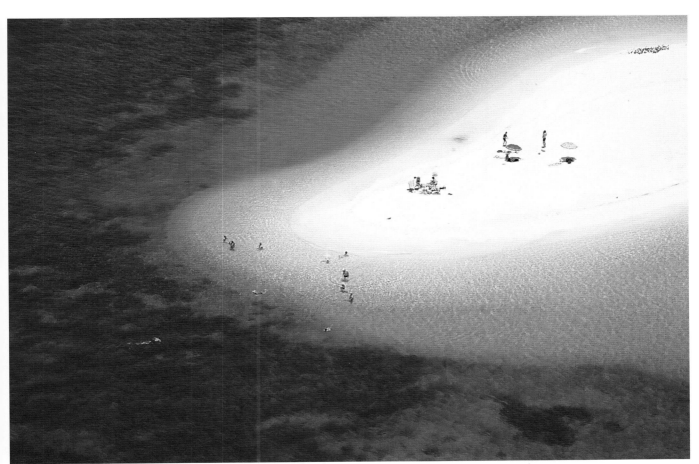

People can swim, snorkel and dive at Beaver Cay – or simply relax.

even getting your feet wet.

For experienced divers there are guided scuba dives at Beaver Cay. These are provided – along with all equipment – by Quickcat Dive Adventures who are based next to the Water Sports centre on Dunk Island. Underwater cameras can also be hired.

People who have never dived before can also learn – or take a single "introductory dive" under the expert supervision of a professional instructor.

Average visibility at Beaver Cay is 12 to 20 metres – and you will see an abundance of beautifully coloured Staghorn coral which is home to myriads of Anthias fish, Damsels, Butterfly and Angel fish.

Feather Stars can be seen in a huge variety of colours. Blue Linkia Starfish adorn the shallower reef areas together with a large selection of sea cucumbers, Pincushion Starfish, Brittle Starfish and Giant clams.

Clown fish and colourful Wrasse are common, and sometimes you will see large Cow Tail and Bull Rays with a 1.5 metre wingspan. Harmless Reef sharks, Manta Rays and turtles can also be seen gliding by on occasions.

Colourful Gorgonian Sea Fans and Giant Whip corals are common in areas of stronger current, and on the northern side of the cay huge black coral trees can be found – a rare sight in such shallow water (12 metres).

"M.V. Hooker" at Taylor Cay.

An unforgettable experience – hand-feeding fish.

The crystal clear water at Taylor Reef is perfect for snorkelling.

Some of the more common fish that make Beaver Cay and the surrounding reef their home are Coral Trout, Rock Cod, Sting Rays, Surgeon fish, Blennies and Gobies, colourful Parrot fish and Moorish Idols.

Underneath the "Quickcat" lie large schools of Spangled Emperor and yellow tailed Fusiliers which wait hungrily to be hand-fed tit-bits by divers.

Another day that is highly recommended is aboard the 40' game-fishing boat "M.V. Hooker". It also travels out to Beaver Cay and nearby Taylor Cay.

On the way you can try your hand at game-fishing – and depending on the time of year you can expect to do battle with

Marlin, Sailfish, Tuna and Spanish Mackerel.

Once you arrive at the Outer Reef you can use hand-lines to haul up fresh Coral Trout, Red Emperor, Sweetlip and Trevally for your evening meal!

At Beaver and Taylor Cay you also have the chance to snorkel – and hand-feed fish.

"M.V. Hooker" is available for private charter or you can join a small party aboard for a great day on and in the water.

Another spectacular way of seeing the Reef is from the air. Small aircraft operate from the Dunk Island airstrip – and the scenic flights they offer over the Reef and the Family Group of Islands should not be missed.

Few people go home without catching their dinner!

An Annual Fishing Tournament.

Fishing in the Great Barrier Reef region can be an unforgettable experience – and each year, during the month of September, Dunk Island plays host to a game-fishing tournament.

Known as the Dunk Island Billfish Classic, it attracts more than 50 game-boats and game anglers from Australia and overseas, all hoping to land record Marlin and Sailfish.

Naturally, demand for accommodation in this period is heavy so if you wish to join in on the action you should book well ahead. Entry forms and details for the tournament can be obtained from most travel agents or through the resort itself. The resort can arrange charter boats for this event as well.

The odd looking Trumpet Fish is a relative of the Sea-horse.

The vibrantly coloured Surgeon Fish is usually found in small schools.

A Nudibranch drifting at night.

A brightly coloured Harlequin Tuskfish.

Clownfish, immune to the stinging tentacles of anemones, hide amongst them for protection.

A variety of coral fish forage for food.

BY THE SAME AUTHOR

THIS book is the most comprehensive guide ever produced for those people who wish to visit Australia's most spectacular region, the Great Barrier Reef.

In addition to covering the incredible underwater life of the Reef and its rich history, this book gives you all the information you need to fully appreciate and visit any of the 18 islands where accommodation is available.

The magnificent fauna and flora of each island is shown and described along with all walking trails and beaches. The book informs you of the trips available from each island to outer reefs, other islands and coral cays. It also tells you the best places to dive, snorkel and fish.

All the resorts and their facilities are covered (there are even examples of the dishes on their restaurant menus).

This 248-page volume also shows the beauty of The Great Barrier Reef region in a way never captured before – through over 400 photographs taken from land, sea and air.

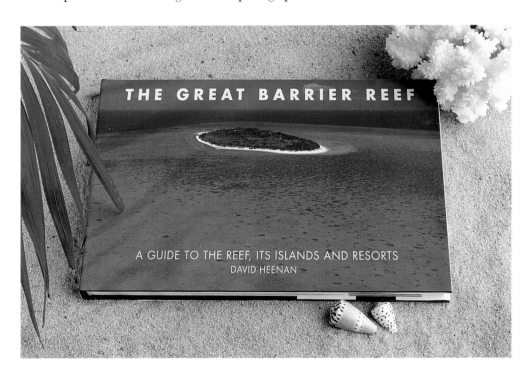

"The most comprehensive guide to be published on the Reef and the islands... a stunning work of literature and photography."
THE SYDNEY MORNING HERALD

"A lavish and definitive guide."
THE MELBOURNE AGE

"If you are serious about your vacation... it is a 'must' investment."
THE CAIRNS POST

To order your copy – personally signed by the author – simply forward a cheque or postal order for $Aus45 (which includes postage and handling) to: Glenmede Pty. Ltd., P.O. Box 291, Red Hill, Queensland, Australia, 4059.